The Secrets of
TUTANKHAMEN'S TOMB

The Secrets of

TUTANKHAMEN'S TOMB

by Leonard Cottrell

Drawings by Raymond Cruz

New York Graphic Society Publishers, Ltd.
Greenwich, Connecticut

The author and publisher wish to express thanks to the
Cooper Square Publishers, Inc. for permission to use
selections from THE TOMB OF TUT-ANKH-AMEN
by Howard Carter and A. C. Mace.
All photos used in this book are copyright © Ashmolean
Museum, Oxford, England and are used with the permission of the Museum.

Library of Congress Catalog Card Number: 64–20445
Text copyright © 1964 by *Leonard Cottrell*
Drawing copyright © 1964 by *New York Graphic Society*

First edition

Published simultaneously in Canada by
McClelland & Stewart, Ltd., Toronto

Printed and bound in the United States of America

*To all young people
who want to be archaeologists*

Contents

The Secrets of
TUTANKHAMEN'S TOMB

One

The Valley of the Kings

Near the little town of Luxor, some six hundred miles up the river Nile, in Upper Egypt, lies a lonely valley. The rocky hills which surround it are not very high, though their dramatic shapes, stark against the blue sky, make them look bigger than they are. There is no river running through the valley; there are no trees or bushes, not even a flower. The landscape is as barren as a crater on the moon. Such beauty as the valley possesses comes mainly from the quality of its color and the varying light which plays upon it. At midday in summer the towering cliffs fling back a fierce glare which makes the traveler half close his eyes. In early morning and late afternoon the valley is pure gold, except in the shadowed clefts where the colors range from russet to deep purple.

At the highest point rises a mountain shaped like a pyramid, which at dawn catches the morning sun while the rest of the valley is still in shadow. To the Ancient Egyptians this was the home of a goddess, *Merit-Segert*, the "Lover of Silence." An ancient saying reads "Beware the

11

Goddess of the Western Peak . . . she strikes instantly and without warning." But when you look more closely at the valley you notice something unusual. At intervals along the steep cliffs, or among mounds of sand and rock lower down, are gaping holes; some are small apertures, others have monumental gateways leading to shafts cut into the hillside. These are the entrances to tombs which were made between thirty-five hundred and three thousand years ago, a period during which the Pharaohs, or kings, of Ancient Egypt ruled over a great empire and enjoyed enormous wealth. Each one, when he died, was buried in a magnificent tomb hollowed out of the mountain. Some of these sepulchers were hundreds of feet deep; long galleries were hewn out of the rock leading to chamber after chamber until at last they opened onto the "Golden Hall," where the body of the Pharaoh lay in the full panoply of his greatness, enclosed in a golden coffin which, in turn, nested within other larger coffins, elaborately inlaid with semiprecious stones.

Around these coffins was built a series of wooden structures, like huge boxes, also plated with thick gold. And in adjoining rock-cut rooms would be all the things which the Pharaoh (who was also a god) would need in the afterlife: his rich furniture, beds, chairs, tables, chests, his royal chariots for hunting and warfare; his weapons,

1. Sketch map of Egypt.

clothing, even games—one of them rather like chess—
with which to while away his leisure time. And, of course,
an abundance of food and wine. For the Ancient Egyptians believed that their kings and other great ones would
need, in the afterlife, all the possessions which had made
their lives enjoyable on earth. Not only that; the soul,
spirit, or *ka* (as they called it) of the dead Pharaoh could
not survive to enjoy life beyond the grave unless his
earthly body was preserved against violation and decay.
That was why they buried the royal bodies in these deep,
elaborate tombs, and why they went to such trouble and
expense to embalm them against decay, and protect them
from robbers.

Yet they failed.

Despite all these precautions—the deep shafts, concealed entrances, "puzzle-passages," blind alleys designed
to fool robbers—despite the ponderous stone sarcophagi
weighing many tons, and the lonely remoteness of the
Royal Valley itself, its watchful priests and guardian sol-
diers, the robbers got through. When the kingdom was
strong and the Valley well guarded, the dead Pharaohs
were reasonably secure. But there came times when weak
rulers and corrupt officials gave the cunning and deter-
mined tomb robbers their chance. How they did it we do
not know, but most probably they bribed the guards and
then tunneled, at night, through tons of rubble filling the

passages until they reached the burial chamber and its rich contents. In doing this the plunderers showed great courage. Not only were they risking being caught, but they were violating the sepulcher of a deity, for to them the dead Pharaoh was a god. Yet they did it, not once but repeatedly. We know this because, by a lucky chance, actual documents have survived, dating from before 1000 B.C., setting down the evidence given by the tomb-robbing gangs when they were brought for trial. Here is a statement by one of the robbers, Amenpnufer:

We went to rob the tombs in accordance with our regular habit, and we found the pyramid of Sekhemre-shedtaui, the son of Re, Sebeksaf, this not being at all like the pyramids and tombs of the nobles which we habitually went to rob. . . . When we broke through the rubble . . . we found this God lying at the back of his burial place. And we found the burial place of Nubkhaas, his queen, situated beside him. . . . We opened their sarcophagi and their coffins in which they were, and found the noble mummy of this King equipped with a falchion [a type of sword]. . . . The noble mummy of this King was completely bedecked with gold, and his coffins were adorned with gold and silver inside and out. . . . We collected the gold we found on the noble mummy of this God . . . and we collected

all that we found on her likewise; and we set fire
to their coffins. We took their furniture, articles
of gold, silver and bronze, and divided them among
ourselves.

The sepulcher of Sebeksaf was that of a relatively minor
king, so one may imagine how such mighty rulers as
Sethos I, Ramesses II and others were equipped.

Robberies like this were so frequent that a time came
when the priests responsible for guarding the Royal Valley despaired of protecting the bodies of the Pharaohs in
their original tombs. So they hit on a desperate and in-
genious plan. One night—it must have been at night to
avoid detection—they secretly gathered together some
thirty royal and princely mummies, took them from their
own tombs, carried them up a steep mountain track and
lowered them, one by one, into a deep rock-cut shaft on
the eastern side of the Theban cliffs—in a cleft facing the
Nile.

At the foot of this deep hole a horizontal shaft ran for
some distance into the rock, ending in a chamber. Within
this chamber the royal bodies—some of which had been
rewrapped several times—were placed in orderly rows.
To most of them the priests attached little labels inscribed
with the name of the king, queen, or prince, sometimes
stating how many times the body had been removed.
These priestly officials were orderly and systematic. It

must have annoyed them greatly to have seen the royal tombs robbed again and again, the bodies unceremoniously tumbled out of their coffins, the mummy wrappings stripped, the furniture stolen, and the priests left to tidy up the mess. So they were careful to attach to each of the bodies a neatly written label giving its history.

We have no written record of this operation, but in 1881 an archaeologist named Emil Brughsch came upon this secret burial place, to which he had been guided by Arab tomb robbers who had already discovered and partially plundered it. In fact they would have stolen all the bodies but for the fact that it would have been impossible to conceal the operation from the eyes of the Egyptian Department of Antiquities. Thus the priests' three-thousand-year-old secret was revealed at last; their ruse had, most astonishingly, been successful, and the Pharaohs had slept in peace for thirty centuries.

Among the royal bodies found in the cache were some of the greatest Pharaohs of Ancient Egypt: such men as Sethos I, Ramesses II, Amenophis I, Tuthmosis I, II and III. In all, as Brughsch wrote at the time: "thirty-six coffins, all belonging to Kings or Queens or Princesses." Only one was found in his original tomb, and that was Amenophis II. Some years later a French archaeologist named Loret discovered the tomb of this great monarch in the Royal Valley. It had, of course, been robbed in ancient times; little furniture was left, but the tomb had been

utilized by the priests as a second repository for royal
bodies. There lay Amenophis II the warrior king, in his
original sarcophagus, and beside him rested the great bow
which, according to an inscription, he had boasted that
only he could draw. With him were twelve more royal
bodies, including Merenptah, thought by some scholars to
have been the Pharaoh of the Exodus who was drowned
in the Red Sea. But there he was, together with Tuthmosis
IV and his son Amenophis III, the father of the famous
"Heretic King" Akhenaten.

At first it was decided to let Amenophis II rest in his
original tomb, together with his bow and a beautiful funerary boat. But not for long. The modern successors of
the Ancient Egyptian tomb robbers would not leave the
tomb alone. The Chief Inspector at Luxor—the man responsible for guarding and protecting the antiquities—was
a young Englishman named Howard Carter. When he
entered the newly plundered tomb of Amenophis II, he
found that the body had been stripped and tossed onto the
floor, and what remained of the funerary furniture had
been stolen. The guards told him that they had been over-
powered by a gang of armed robbers. Carter wrote at the
time:

> The bandages had been ripped open, but the body
> not broken. This had evidently been done by an
> expert, as only the pieces where objects are usually

found had been touched. The boat in the antechamber had been stolen, the mummy that was upon it was lying on the floor and had been smashed to pieces. I carefully examined the wrappings of the royal mummy to see if there were any signs of their having contained jewellery, but could find no trace.

In fact, the ancient Egyptian tomb robbers, who had plundered the same sepulcher some three thousand years earlier, had left nothing for their modern successors to find.

Discoveries such as this, made toward the end of the last century, inspired other explorers to dig in the Valley. Admittedly most of the great tombs had been robbed—indeed, more than twenty of them had been tourist attractions as far back as Greek and Roman times, between twenty-five hundred and two thousand years ago. Greek and Roman tourists used to inscribe their initials on the walls, where they can still be seen, while the smoke of their torches has blackened the roofs of the empty sepulchers. Yet there existed lists of Pharaohs, kept by the priests, and in these lists were names of one or two kings not yet accounted for. Perhaps there was a faint chance that one or two of these tombs had been overlooked by the robbers?

So archaeologists, professional and amateur, came to the Valley, dug and redug, combing the barren cliffs from end to end, excavating hundreds of tons of rock and sand, but with sparse results. Loret was the most fortunate discoverer. After him came an American named Theodore Davis who, in 1903, came upon the tomb of two Theban nobles, Prince Yuya and his wife Thuya, a find which yielded specimens of chariots and other funerary furniture—the best-preserved examples found up to that date. Four years later Davis, assisted by an archaeologist named Ayrton, found another small rock-cut tomb containing a large gilded wooden shrine, much damaged, with a damaged coffin containing the body of a young man. The tomb was dated toward the end of the Eighteenth Dynasty (1555–1350 B.C.); the gilded shrine was inscribed with the name of Queen Tiye—wife of Amenophis III and mother of Akhenaten; but no one has yet decided to whom the coffin belonged, or the name of the young man inside it.

That appeared to be the end of the great discoveries. Davis went on digging, year after year, but without result. In 1914, at the outbreak of the First World War, he relinquished the concession granted to him by the Egyptian Government and stated candidly that, in his opinion, no more royal tombs would ever be found. The Royal Valley had been exhausted.

Two

The Discoverers

When young Howard Carter came to Egypt for the first time he was eighteen. Normally he could never have afforded the cost of the trip from England, for his father was a struggling artist who painted portraits of animals. This may seem a strange pursuit, but in those days— some seventy years ago—English gentlemen, fond of riding and hunting, used to commission painters to make portraits of their favorite horses. This was how Mr. Carter senior made his living. Young Howard seems to have inherited the gift, and after leaving school he obtained part-time work copying pictures and inscriptions brought back from Egypt by Egyptologists. One of these scholars, the late Professor Newberry, admired Carter's gifts so much that he arranged to pay his fare and expenses to Egypt so that he could copy certain paintings in the tombs at Beni Hasan.

Howard, a very bright London boy, fell in love with Egypt, as many have done before and since his time. He had a good ear for languages, soon learned sufficient Ar-

abic to get by, and plunged himself wholeheartedly into
this exciting world of Egyptology. He had the advantage
of working with scholars, but he also read deeply and
widely, to such good effect that in time he obtained a
minor post in the Department of Antiquities of the Egyptian Government, the department which is responsible for
protecting the antiquities of the Nile Valley and sometimes conducting excavations. But Howard Carter had another greater advantage. He was good with his hands; he
had an extraordinary practical skill in excavating and preserving frail objects of antiquity. Also he knew the peas-
ants of Upper Egypt, where he was stationed. These men,
many of whom lived on the site of the ancient tombs, had
for generations made a skilled profession of tomb-robbery,
and "illicit digging." Into the constant battle of wits between them and the Department of Antiquities, Carter
entered with zest. In his job he had to be not only an
archaeologist, but also a policeman and detective. For instance, in the previous chapter I mentioned that the tomb
of Amenophis II was robbed, and that the guards stated
that they had been overcome by armed intruders. But
Carter was suspicious. Inspecting the padlock, he found it
had been "fixed" with silver paper so that it appeared to
be locked though it was not. Later he traced the actual
robber by the imprint of his sandals on the dusty floor of
the tomb. The man belonged to the notorious family of

Abderassul, the same which had discovered the famous burial cache of the Pharaohs at Deir el Bahari.

On another occasion, having had wind of the fact that certain men were going to make an attack on the tomb of Queen Hatshepsut, high up in the Theban cliffs, Carter and his guards laid in wait for them at night, and in the

2. *Detail from the little gold-plated shrine in which Tutankhamen draws a bow while seated on a folding stool. He is accompanied by his wife and tame lion.*

brisk gun battle which ensued the robbers were driven off. Carter did his job well; he instituted a system of reliable guardians, called *ghaffirs;* he protected the principal tombs with iron gates, and took other precautions which at least minimized illegal digging for antiquities and the defacing of tomb sculptures. For by this time—the beginning of the century—interest in Ancient Egypt had reached a point at which art dealers were prepared to pay high prices for a piece of sculpture hacked from the wall of a tomb, and the genial desperados of El Gournah (the Arab village built in the ancient cemetery) were always ready to supply this demand. They even sank holes in the floors of their huts and built passages leading to the tombs!

Eventually Carter was appointed Chief Inspector of the Theban Necropolis—a splendid-sounding title which is still held by the modern occupant of the position. This official is responsible for guarding and preserving the richest and most important archaeological site in Egypt, which includes not only the Valley of the Kings but the numerous tombs of the nobles and high officers of Pharaoh built in the cliffs facing the Nile. The Chief Inspector also carried out important excavations. Sometimes there were wealthy foreign amateurs who enjoyed wintering in Luxor, and who became interested in Egyptology and were prepared to finance excavations. Among these was Theodore Davis, who had worked on the tomb of Yuya and Thuya in 1903 but after twelve years' excavation had decided that the Royal Valley had been combed clean. When he relinquished the concession granted to him by the Egyptian Government, it was taken up by a new amateur archaeologist, Lord Carnarvon. Since the Egyptian authorities took care that actual archaeological work was supervised by professionals, Howard Carter was "assigned" to Lord Carnarvon.

There could hardly be a greater contrast than that between Carter and Carnarvon—between the almost self-taught professional archaeologist and the English aristocrat to whom Egyptology was a hobby. Apart from his salary Carter had no money; Carnavon was a man of high birth and considerable wealth. And excavation—even in those days—was an expensive business. It had to be carried out systematically over a period of years, and beside the wages of the numerous workmen there would often be the salaries of specialists called in if an important discovery was made. Carnavon financed the excavation of the Royal Valley, and of course took a close interest in it. But it was Carter who, from his long experience, selected the sites to be dug, and supervised the work. Excavation was normally carried out only from autumn to early spring; in summer the weather became too hot.

Owing to the outbreak of the First World War, not much excavation was carried out until 1917, but from then onward, for five years, Carter and Carnarvon patiently explored, moving hundreds of tons of earth left by previous investigators, redigging sites which had already been dug on the off chance that a tomb entrance had been overlooked in that tumbled wilderness of sand and rock chippings. It seemed a forlorn hope, but they went on, year after year, even though Sir Gaston Maspero, the Director of the Antiquities Department, agreed with Davis that the Valley had been exhausted.

Eventually, by the end of the 1921 season, Carnarvon decided to give up. During the summer of 1922, when both men were back in England, Lord Carnarvon invited Carter to his country home, Highclere Castle and informed him that, in view of the expense of excavation, and the fruitless results of their joint labors, he had decided to discontinue further excavation. Carter understood and shared his patron's disappointment, but pleaded with him to continue for one more season. There were two main reasons, he said, why he wished to do this. First, in the previous year, 1921, he had come upon a small, shallow pit containing a few scraps of fabric and some jar sealings bearing the name of Tutankhamen, a Pharaoh whose tomb had never been found. He was not an important king and had reigned for only a few years. Still he was a Pharaoh; his name was on the "King-lists" kept by the ancient priests, and the presence of these scraps of fabric and jar sealings, which might have been connected with a funeral ceremony, suggested to Carter that the tomb might be found nearby. Carnarvon was skeptical.

Carter then produced the well-worn map of the Royal Valley which they had used for so many seasons. They had worked systematically, combing the Valley foot by foot, and as each area had been cleared and nothing found, that area was marked off on the map. But, Carter pointed out, there was still one small triangular area, covered with sand and rock chippings, which had not been cleared, partly because it was immediately in front of the well-known empty tomb of Ramesses VI which was frequently visited by tourists. Twice before Carter had proposed digging in this area but had stopped. On the first occasion he had been working for Theodore Davis, who had suggested that he shift to a more favorable spot. On the second he had decided to reserve clearance for a time when there would be no interference from visitors. Carter declared that once he had satisfied himself that the twice-overlooked site concealed nothing, he too would be convinced that further work was futile. Would Carnarvon please finance one more season's excavation?

To Carter's intense relief his patron agreed, and the two men parted, Carter to return to Egypt, while Carnarvon stayed in England until he was ready to join his colleague.

On October 28, 1922, Carter was back in the little town of Luxor, re-enrolling his workmen for what he believed would be his last season's excavation for Carnarvon. On November 1 he was back in the mysterious Valley. There lay the great mounds of chippings left by previous excavators, and there, like black mouths in the cliffs, gaped the entrances to the plundered tombs of thirty Pharaohs, seeming to mock the efforts of the archaeologist. Carter and his men began systematically to clear the area in front of the tomb of Ramesses VI. What happened four days later is best described in Carter's own words:

> By late afternoon of the third, my men had laid bare the foundation stones of a row of ancient workmens' huts beneath which we had never probed. Hardly had I arrived . . . the next morning, than the unusual silence, due to the stoppage of work, made me realise that something out of ordinary had happened. . . . The workmen had discovered a step cut in the rock immediately under the first hut to be attacked. It seemed almost too good to be true, but a short amount of extra clearing revealed the fact that we were actually in the entrance of a steep cut in the rock some thirteen feet below the entrance to the tomb of Ramesses VI. (See Fig. I).

That step was the first of sixteen leading down into the

rock. At the bottom was a blocked doorway. There was no plunderers' hole in the blocking as in so many similar entrances. Moreover, impressed in the cement which covered the blocking stones were the seals of the Necropolis priests, placed there some three thousand years ago. The seals showed the familiar sign of the Royal Necropolis "the jackal and nine captives," but Carter could find no seal indicating the tomb's owner. Nevertheless two facts were clear: (a) the tomb must have belonged to someone of importance—because of the royal seal—and (b) the door could not have been opened since, at the latest, the time of the Twentieth Dynasty (1200–1090 B.C.) because the workmen's huts, which screened the entrance from above, were of that date. Carter wrote:

> It was a thrilling moment. Alone, save for my native workmen, I found myself after years of comparatively unproductive labour on the threshold of what might prove to be a magnificent discovery. Anything, literally anything might lie beyond that passage, and it needed all my self-control to keep from breaking down the doorway and investigating then and there.

But Carter refilled the entrance stairway again, mounted a strong guard over it, and recrossed the Nile to the telegraph office. Later that day the distinguished archaeologist Sir Alan Gardiner was just sitting down to dinner at his home in England when the telephone rang. Lord Carnarvon was on the line. "Listen to this," he said. "I've just had a wire from Carter. It reads 'At last you have made wonderful discovery in Valley; a magnificent tomb with seals intact; re-covered same for your arrival. Congratulations. Carter.'"

Lord Carnarvon, accompanied by his daughter, Lady Evelyn Herbert, went out to Egypt as quickly as possible, and joined Carter at Luxor on November 23. Carnarvon had asked Sir Alan Gardiner, the distinguished philologist, to go with them, since if the tomb was that of the missing Pharaoh, Tutankhamen, it would probably contain inscriptions which would interest Gardiner. But Sir Alan wished to spend Christmas at home with his children and did not go out until early in the following year.

On the afternoon of the twenty-fourth, the staircase having again been completely cleared, Carter found something which had been invisible before. Besides the familiar Necropolis seal of the "jackal and nine captives" were others, and these bore the unmistakable name of Tutankhamen. This raised the excavator's hopes, but there was another, disquieting discovery. Careful examination of the doorway showed that it had been *twice* opened and resealed in ancient times, and the Necropolis seal was on the reclosed part of the door. Therefore the tomb was probably not intact, as Carter had hoped. The resealing was clear evidence that at some remote time thieves had entered it; later it had been reclosed by the priests.

The decisive moment had arrived.

> With trembling hands (wrote Carter) I made a tiny breach in the upper left-hand corner. Darkness and blank space, as far as an iron testing-rod could reach. . . . Candle tests were applied as a precaution against possible foul gases, and then, widening the hole a little, I inserted the candle

3. The cover for an alabaster bowl, found in Tutankhamen's tomb. The bowl in which the bird sits is also of alabaster; the bird is carved in painted and stuccoed wood, the tongue of ivory stained red.

and peered in, Lord Carnarvon, Lady Evelyn
Herbert and Callender [Mr. A. R. Callender, one
of Carter's assistants] standing anxiously beside me
to hear the verdict. At first I could see nothing, the
hot air escaping from the chamber causing the
candle to flicker. But presently, as my eyes grew
accustomed to the light, details of the room
emerged slowly from the mist, strange animals,
statues, and gold—everywhere the glint of gold.
For a moment—an eternity it must have seemed to
the others standing by, I was struck dumb; then
Lord Carnarvon inquired anxiously—"Can you see
anything?"

"Yes," I replied, . . . wonderful things. . . ."

Three

The Pharaoh's Treasure

The news of this discovery, flashed across the world, had an impact such as no archaeological find has ever made. The press of the world sent their reporters hotfoot to Luxor; visitors packed the hotels, and suddenly Carnarvon and Carter, who had been carrying on their work quietly for five years, found themselves internationally known figures. The presence of so many visitors was embarrassing, for Carter was about to perform one of the most difficult, delicate, and responsible tasks ever entrusted to an archaeologist. He was not at the best of times an even-tempered man, and the additional strain frayed his nerves almost beyond endurance. Quarrels ensued, even between Carter and his friend and patron, Lord Carnarvon, chiefly over what should be done with the treasures which the tomb contained. Carter believed that they should go to the Department of Antiquities of the Egyptian Government. Carnarvon, who had financed the discovery, believed he had a right to retain at least some of the objects.

It is not the purpose of this book to enter into these arguments; they are only mentioned to illustrate the emotional atmosphere in which the clearing of the tomb was conducted, at least in the early days. Carter once remarked bitterly that it was like asking a surgeon to conduct a critical operation with the press of the world jogging his elbow. And the operation certainly was critical. Carter had found what appeared to be the only intact—or reasonably intact—tomb of a Pharaoh ever found; it was probably the only example which would ever be found. Within that outer chamber—already glimpsed by Carter —lay scores of precious, unique objects, the funerary equipment of a king who had died more than three thousand years ago.

For thirty centuries they had been sealed in an airtight chamber—objects made of inlaid wood, gold, silver and semiprecious stones. How were they to be preserved intact? Would some of them disintegrate when exposed to the outer air? Could this be prevented? What were the best chemical methods to use? Above all, to Carter, as to all serious archaeologists, archaeology was a search for knowledge and not a mere treasure hunt. Therefore, whatever happened, means *must* be found of recording accurately the objects, the positions in which they were found, and, with the aid of specialists, of gleaning every bit of information this unique discovery might yield. It had to be a team job; there must be someone to undertake

the photography, a botanist to examine the plant specimens, a philologist to deal with the inscriptions, chemists
to advise on the best way of preserving fragile objects, especially those of wool and fabric, and so on. But Carter
was the leader and inspirer of the team. Gardiner says of
him:

> He had a lot to contend with—official interference,
> irritating delays, misunderstanding and a surfeit of
> unwelcome publicity, and perhaps he was not the
> best-tempered of men. But he was a superb
> draughtsman. He was nearly a genius in the practi-
> cal mechanics of excavation, and in the recording
> and preservation of fragile objects of antiquity. But
> his greatest gift was patience.

The outer, sealed door opened into the first of several
chambers. Let us listen to another voice—that of the late
Professor James Breasted, describing the scene when the
blocking was completely removed and the excavators
were able to enter the Antechamber—the first human
beings to tread that floor since about 1400 B.C.

> We saw an incredible vision . . . an impossible
> scene from a fairy-tale, an enchanted property-
> room from an opera house of some great com-
> poser's dreams. Opposite us were three couches on
> which the King had lain, all about us were chests,

caskets, alabaster vases, gold-embellished stools and chairs—the heaped-up riches of a Pharaoh who had died . . . before Crete had passed her zenith, before Greece had been born or Rome conceived, or more than half the history of civilisation had taken place. . . . Against the white limestone wall, the colours of all these things were vibrant yet soft—a medley of brown, yellow, blue, amber, gold, russet and black.[1]

The Antechamber, as Carter called it, was not very large, much smaller than the chambers in most Egyptian royal sepulchers, but it was crammed with objects piled up in no sort of order. (See Figs. II and III). In fact Gardiner said they looked like furniture in a warehouse, tidily arranged, but without any regard for artistic grouping—except for two items, and these immediately riveted the attention of the explorers. At the far end of the crowded chamber stood two life-size figures of wood, colored black and gold, and each wearing on its forehead the golden uraeus—sign of royalty; each carried in its right hand a gold

4. One of the two lifesize statues of Tutankhamen which faced each other on each side of the walled-up entrance to the funerary chamber. Both are made of wood covered with black resin. The eyes and eyebrows are made of gold, the uraeus (headdress) and sandals are gilded.

[1] Breasted, Charles, *Pioneer to the Past*, Charles Scribner's Sons, New York, 1943.

wand of office. Between these two guardian figures Carter and his colleagues saw yet another blocked doorway, also bearing the seals of the Royal Necropolis. "Behind the sealed door there were to be other chambers, perhaps a succession of them, and in one of them beyond the shadow of doubt, we should see the Pharaoh lying."

When the archaeologists had recovered a little from their first bewilderment and wonder, they began a systematic examination of the Antechamber, and soon they noticed something else. Everywhere there was evidence of a hasty tidying-up. Not all the objects were intact. Thieves must have entered and been interrupted before they could do much damage. They had, however, opened one of the King's wooden chests and tumbled articles of his clothing onto the floor. The priests who tidied the tomb had stuffed these garments back into their boxes without bothering to fold them properly and had mixed up with them small objects which clearly belonged in other boxes. The gold struts under the seats of one of the royal thrones were missing, probably broken off by the thieves who must have worked in desperate haste, grabbing what they could. One of the plunderers had gathered together a handful of golden rings and then had to fling it down in his retreat. To the left of the doorway, under one of the gold-encased wooden couches, was the open entrance to yet another, smaller chamber, on the floor of which still lay objects scattered in confusion by the thieves.

Yet very little of importance was missing or damaged. It was a miracle, but there could be no doubt that since that abortive raid, made some three thousand years ago, no one had entered the Tomb of Tutankhamen. Alone

5. Plan of the tomb and identification of the rooms at the time of the discovery.

among all the Pharaohs of Egypt's Imperial Age he had slept securely in his original sepulcher and was, in fact, still sleeping behind that blocked door guarded by the two sentinel figures.

It was here that Carter's patience showed itself. The temptation to break down that door and see what lay beyond must have been extremely strong; but he resisted it, resolving first to clear the Antechamber and the small annex to it, taking every possible care to preserve the multitude of objects they contained. In order to do this he and Carnarvon gathered around them a team of experts, all of whom deserve honor for the work they did. There was Albert M. Lythgoe, then Curator of the Egyptian Department of the Metropolitan Museum of Art, New York; Herbert E. Winlock and Arthur C. Mace, also from the Metropolitan Museum. Professor Percy Newberry was called in to help in identifying the wreaths and other plants found in the tomb; Sir Alan Gardiner was to examine the inscriptions, if any were found. There was Harry Burton, the photographer; Hall and Hauser, draughtsmen; and A. Lucas, Director of the Chemical Department of the Egyptian Government, who gave of his vast experience in the protection and preservation of Egyptian antiquities. The preliminary work took two months. Carter wrote:

> It was slow work, painfully slow, and nerve-racking at that, for one felt all the time a heavy

weight of responsibility. Every excavator must, if
he has any archaeological conscience at all. . . . The
things he finds are not his own property to treat as
he pleases. They are a strict legacy from the past
to the present age, and if by carelessness, slackness
or ignorance he lessens the sum of knowledge that
might have been obtained from them he knows
himself to be guilty of an archaeological crime.

The largest tomb in the Royal Valley is that of Sethos I,
which has many spacious galleries and chambers. Carter
obtained permission to have it temporarily closed to visitors so that he could use it as a laboratory and workshop.
In this way each object, as it was removed from Tutankhamen's tomb, could be first taken to the laboratory for
treatment before being packed for transport to Cairo, six
hundred miles away. Every day huge throngs of visitors
and journalists hung around the Valley, hoping to see
some new object removed from the tomb to the laboratory. It was the only chance which most of the news-
papermen had of seeing the objects, for reasons which will
appear later, and which caused much bitterness. Carter
and his colleagues worked through the long hot days,
and often far into the night, in the lamplit interior of
Sethos's tomb. Every article was photographed, drawn,
and recorded in Carter's precise handwriting on index-file
cards which can still be seen at the Griffith Institute,
Oxford.

In the next chapter we shall examine some of the more wonderful of those objects, but meanwhile we must pause to describe briefly some of the difficulties which dogged Carter and his team during that first, exhausting season, and the atmosphere of frantic sensationalism which surrounded it.

One newspaper, the London *Daily Telegraph* thus described the scene on January 25, 1923:

> The scene . . . awakened memories of Derby Day. The road leading to the rock-enclosed ravine . . . was packed with vehicles and animals of every conceivable variety. The guides, donkey-boys, sellers of antiquities, and hawkers of lemonade were doing a roaring trade. . . . When the last article had been removed from the corridor today the newspaper correspondents began a spirited dash across the desert to the banks of the Nile on donkeys, horses, camels and chariot-like sand-carts in a race to be the first to reach the telegraph offices.

This was bad enough, but the throngs of visitors made matters even worse. "There were days," wrote Carter, "in which we actually had ten parties of visitors, and if we had given way to every demand there would not have been a day in which we did not exceed the ten. In other words there would have been weeks and weeks at a time when no work would have been done at all." As a result of the archaeologists' firmness in limiting these unwelcome visits, they were accused of selfishness, bad manners, even boorishness; yet, if Carter had admitted more than a limited number of people to the tomb at a time, there was a grave danger that some of the precious things would have been damaged.

Carnarvon, in his turn, was attacked in the press for having made the *Times* of London his sole agent for the distribution of news. Naturally the other newspapers were furious. One of their correspondents wrote of Carnarvon:

> . . . the tomb is not his private property. He had not dug up the bones of his ancestors in the Welsh mountains. He has stumbled on a Pharaoh in the land of the Egyptians . . . by making an exclusive secret of the contents of the inner tomb he has ranged against him the majority of the world's most influential newspapers.

This was, unfortunately, true. But in fact Carnarvon was trying to protect his colleagues and himself from the necessity of coping with scores of journalists when every ounce of concentration was needed for their own unique task. This strained, tense atmosphere grew with the passing months, and eventually led to actions which might well have wrecked the greatest archaeological discovery ever made in Egypt. Meanwhile let us look more closely at the things which, day after day, Carter's workmen were removing from the Antechamber.

6. *This likeness of the king, in painted and stuccoed wood, was long thought to be a "dummy" of Tutankhamen, placed in the tomb to wear his robes and necklaces.*

Four

Desperation and Defeat

Clearing of the Antechamber began on December 27, 1922, and was not completed until the middle of February, 1923—seven weeks of harassing, nerve-racking work in a room measuring only 25 ft. by 16 ft., containing over six hundred objects, many of them in a fragile condition. Some were so delicate that they had to be chemically treated on the spot, even before they were removed to the laboratory.

As Carter and his colleagues removed these things, one by one, their emotions were pulled first this way, then that. On the one hand it was their duty, as archaeologists, to photograph, record, preserve, and carefully transport each treasure from the tomb to the laboratory and thence to the Cairo Museum. But they were not merely transferring objects from one museum gallery to another; they were moving about in a room which no other human beings had seen for over three thousand years, and as they worked their way systematically from one end to the other, they found clear and dramatic evidence of what their predecessors had been up to. It was all very well to consider this as an intact sepulcher which had lain undisturbed for thirty centuries. It had, indeed, been miraculously preserved, unlike twenty-seven other royal burials in the Valley. But before the priests had sealed the doorway and left the tomb to silence and darkness, there had been some remarkable happenings within those walls.

For instance, one of the first objects to be examined was a brilliantly painted wooden casket (illustrated on page 47). The outer surface had been prepared with gesso (a form of plaster), and on this the Ancient Egyptian artist had depicted lively scenes showing the king hunting wild game, and battle scenes in which Tutankhamen, in his chariot, slays his traditional enemies, the Nubians and the Asiatics. These tableaus, with their delicacy of detail and harmony of color, are reminiscent of Persian miniatures. But when they opened the lid Carter and his colleagues came upon a very odd medley of things.

Usually such boxes contain objects of one type, or at least of related types, but in this painted casket there were a pair of rush and papyrus sandals; a royal robe decorated with gold sequins and elaborate beadwork; other royal robes, one ornamented with three thousand golden rosettes; three more pairs of sandals worked in gold; a gilt headrest; an archer's gauntlet; various rolls and pads of cloth; and some articles of jewelry—all bundled together with the garments, which had not been neatly folded but stuffed into the box willy-nilly.

In another casket was a leopard-skin robe, such as used by priests, decorated with gold and silver stars, a buckle of sheet gold, a solid gold scepter ornamented with lapis-

7. *A detail from the painted chest showing Tut-ankhamen in his chariot, doing battle with his traditional enemies, the Asiatics and Nubians (see Illustration 8).*

8. *The lower end of a ceremonial cane shows the two hereditary enemies of Egypt: the Asiatic Syrian, whose face and hands are of ivory, and the African Nubian, whose arms and head are of ebony.*

lazuli glass, several necklaces, and a handful of heavy gold rings twisted up in a fold of linen. (See Fig. IV). These rings, mentioned in Chapter Three, had evidently formed part of a thief's intended loot. But why had they been put back in this box together with other ill-assorted articles?

Then there was a long ebony box at the top of which, just under the hinged lid, were shirts and underwear, all crumpled together. But underneath were sticks, bows, and a number of arrows, the points of which had been broken off for the sake of the metal. Thieves again. It soon became clear that originally these boxes had been neatly filled with objects of a similar kind; this one, for example, had contained bows and arrows. But when the chamber was tidied up by the priests after the robbers had left, the miscellaneous articles were gathered up from the floor and jammed, higgledy-piggledy, into the nearest available container.

The mounting of one of these sticks (illustrated on page 48) shows two captives, an Asiatic and a Negro— Egypt's traditional enemies of the North and South— bound together by the legs and forming the curved end of a walking stick. Their faces, hands, and feet are of ivory and ebony. Another similar stick has a handle in the form of a bound Negro captive. Some of the boxes still bore the original labels with inscriptions in *hieratic* (the An-

cient Egyptian written form of hieroglyphs), detailing
what was supposed to be inside. One, for instance stated
that the box contained seventeen objects of lapis-lazuli
blue. There were, in fact, sixteen vases inside, but in ad-
dition, carelessly packed, were a couple of boomerangs, a
carved ivory casket, a wine-strainer, and the greater part
of an elaborate corselet.

Everywhere there was evidence of attempted plunder
followed by a hurried repacking and tidying up of the
tomb's contents. The most prominent objects in the Antechamber were three magnificent couches of wood, plated
with gold, ornamented with the heads of animals; a lioness,
a hippopotamus, and a cow. (Two of these are illustrated
on pages 51 and 52). Such heavy furniture could offer
no attraction to the thieves, who had left them alone; but
under one of the couches was something even more
splendid, a glittering throne entirely covered with thick

*9. This funerary bedhead is made of gilded and
stuccoed wood. It is thought to be a lioness because even in Ancient Egypt the royal throne
was sometimes shown carried by lions. The ani-
mal's eyes are of crystal outlined with blue glass-
paste, also used for the nose.*

sheet gold, delicately inlaid with brilliantly colored glass, faience, and semiprecious stones. (You can see it on page 55). The arms are shaped in the form of winged serpents —the royal cobra of Ancient Egypt—each wearing the Double Crown, symbolizing dominion over the South and North.

But what riveted the attention of the archaeologists was the scene inlaid on the back of the throne in red glass, blue faience, and calcite, glowing against a background of sheet gold. It was a scene in one of the rooms of Tutankhamen's palace. The young monarch is resting on a chair very like those found in his tomb. Standing before him his equally young queen, Ankhesenamun, wearing an elaborate beaded collar, a long, elegant, semitransparent robe of pleated linen, and a tall headdress. She leans forward in a tender attitude, gently anointing the king's shoulder with perfumed oil from a vessel she holds in her left hand. The whole scene is charged with affection; these are royal personages, almost weighed down by their trappings. Yet still they are human beings.

The work obviously belongs to what is called the

10. Another of the funerary bedheads shows the goddess Tueris in the form of a hippopotamus. The teeth and tongue are of ivory, with the tongue stained red.

Amarna Period of Egyptian art, a time when the Pharaoh Amenophis IV, who changed his name to Akhenaten, suddenly forbade the worship of the god Amun and the numerous other deities who had been reverenced in Egypt for more than fifteen hundred years. He tried to replace them by one sole god, whom he called the Aten, giver of life, and represented by the sun's disk with descending rays. You can see Akhenaten's god above the young couple. The object on the right is a round table, represented in such a way that you see both the sides and the top at once. The Egyptian artists ignored perspective.

But when Carter examined the legs of the throne, he found that the thieves had again been active. Several of the gold-encased struts had been snapped off; the plunderers would, of course, have taken the entire throne if they had had the chance, but fortunately for us they were prevented. *How* were they prevented? What had happened in that dark, cramped, rock-cut chamber some thirty centuries ago? How had the thieves got in? And having done so, and overturned so much in their frantic search for loot, why had they left so much behind, even to the handful of rings tied up in a piece of the royal linen?

11. The gold-plated throne, inlaid with multicolored glass paste, glazed terracotta and semiprecious stones.

They entered by tunneling a hole through the rubble filling between the outer and inner doorways of the entrance corridor. Carter, long familiar with the habits of thieves, ancient and modern, detected this when he noticed that most of this rubble was clean and untouched, but that at one point, near the ceiling of the corridor the stones were dirty, indicating where the filling had been replaced when the tunnel had been filled in again. Having broken through the second sealed doorway the thieves had found themselves in the Antechamber, from which they had gained entrance to adjoining chambers by making holes in the partition walls.

One hole, in the wall beneath one of the great gilded couches, was still open; it had not been resealed by the Necropolis priests. Through it Carter saw a scene of utter confusion in the little room beyond. Alabaster vases, caskets, weapons, clothing, ornaments, were strewn over the floor and piled high against the walls. On a wooden bow case, still clearly visible, were the actual footprints of one of the thieves. The archaeologists, after a dismayed survey of this room, called the Annexe, decided to postpone its clearance until the last.

Another hole, just wide enough to admit a small man (or woman) had been bored through the sealed entrance leading to the Burial Chamber, between the two sentinel figures. (See Figs. V and VI). Penelope Fox, in her book, *Tutankhamun's Treasure*, remarks:

"A small breach had been made, which may or may not have been re-sealed anciently. . . ."

It is obvious that the thieves, who probably entered the tomb not long after the King's burial, could not have hoped to carry away the larger objects, even if they had had time. The tunnels were too small for that. They were after portable loot, especially precious metal, and they knew where to look for it. Their first action was to open the numerous boxes and toss their contents onto the floor. Then, in a frenzy of fearful haste, they tried to collect everything of value which they could carry away. One man found the gold rings. Snatching up a piece of the royal linen, he twisted the rings within its folds, made a knot, and probably stuffed the loot in his loincloth. Another man tore from its pedestal a small golden statue. A third snapped off the arrowheads, which were of valuable metal, and broke off the golden struts of the royal throne. The beautiful corselet, covered with golden sequins, was torn apart. Perhaps the thieves quarreled and fought, blundering about in the semidarkness, while the watchers at the far end of the tunnel shouted to them to be quick.

Then something happened; exactly what we do not know. Either the robbers were trapped in the tomb by the guardians of the Necropolis, or, interrupted in their plundering, were forced to fly and were pursued. This is not mere speculation. The evidence was all too clear to the archaeologists as they examined the contents of the Antechamber. All that is uncertain is the outcome. The thieves left behind numerous objects of value which they could have taken, such as the gold rings found still wrapped in the scrap of linen in one of the boxes. On the other hand, some objects were missing. There is a strong possibility that some of the thieves got away, but that others were captured and forced to relinquish their loot. Some may have been trapped in the tomb itself, and their subsequent fate could not have been enviable.

Tomb robbers, ancient and modern, are the bane of the Egyptologist. But I suspect that Carter, despite his frustration, may have had a sneaking respect for those desperate men who had preceded him. Spurred on perhaps by hunger and poverty, they had defied not only the power of the state but—even more terrible—their own belief in the sanctity of the God-King, the Pharaoh, and violated his sepulcher. They failed, in this one instance; unhappily for them, but luckily for us.

Five

In the Presence of the King

It might be asked why it was that some of the objects needed artificial preservation whereas others did not. Obviously things made of stone, metal, or glass are less liable to be affected by humidity, dryness, or natural decay. One such is the lovely "Wishing Cup" illustrated on page 60. It is of translucent alabaster, and is called "lotiform" because the handle consists of lotus flowers supporting the emblem of eternal life. The hieroglyphic inscription gives the many titles of Tutankhamen and concludes:

> Live thy *Ka*, and mayst thou spend millions of years, thou lover of Thebes, sitting with thy face to the North Wind, and thine eyes beholding felicity.

The "wish" "mayst thou spend millions of years . . ." is fairly common in Egyptian tombs. The *ka* or spirit of the dead man was expected to spend some time living in the tomb or "House of Eternity." Egypt being a very hot country, one of the greatest pleasures is to sit out of doors in the evening and enjoy the north wind. That is what the King's *ka* wished to do.

To return to the objects in the Antechamber and their state of preservation; the wooden articles, of sound timber and well carpentered, were usually in fair condition, but had shrunk. When they were plated with gold and inlaid with delicate mosaics, this caused difficulty. The shrinkage left a gap between the wood and the covering, the tiny

12. The "Wishing Cup."

pieces of glass, lapis, carnelian etc. tended to break away, and Carter had to resort to melted paraffin wax to hold everything together. It was even worse with the fabrics. If these had been neatly folded before being put in the boxes they might have survived, or at least the gold sequins and other ornaments sewn on to them would have been found in their correct relative positions. But this was rarely the case. The garments had been jammed into the caskets, and mixed up with various items of hardware; humidity (of which we shall speak later) had caused the linen to disintegrate to the point where it fell apart at a touch. Then there were the beads—hundreds of thousands of them—which had been inlaid into the beautiful pectorals (breastplates) and other golden ornaments, or made up the many-tiered necklaces, collarets, and bracelets of which the Egyptians were so fond. Many of these beads were scattered in confusion, but in other cases, by careful scrutiny the archaeologists were able to note and record where they had fallen; then came the tedious operation of stringing them together on new threads.

For certain reasons—partly the seepage of water through the porous rock, partly the decomposition of organic matter within the tomb—dampness had, at some time, attacked some of the objects. For instance at the southern end of the Antechamber, near the door, were the dismembered remains of a number of chariots; the axles had been sawed apart to get the vehicles into the tomb, but the wheels, bodywork and poles were all intact, and richly plated with gold. (See Fig. III). They have since been reconstructed, but the harness had to be replaced. The leather of the original one had decomposed into a black, viscid mass due to humidity.

These chariots (others were found in the Treasury adjoining the burial chamber), were among the most interesting objects found in an Egyptian royal tomb. Many pictures of them existed, and some examples had been found, namely in the tomb of Yuya and Thuya discovered by the American amateur archaeologist, Theodore Davis. But these chariots of Tutankhamen were the first royal examples ever found. His name was on them, of course, together with gold-embossed panels depicting the usual bound Nubian and Asiatic captives. (See illustration on page 63.) The chariot, though used for hunting, was primarily an instrument of war, and a deadly one. Some Pharaohs, such as Ramesses II, led their armies into battle from chariots, and the chariot arm of the Egyptian army was probably roughly equivalent to the swift light-armored tanks of modern times. Its great advantage was mobility. There were two-man chariots, one man driving, the other shooting arrows, but those found in Tutankhamen's tomb seem to have been designed only for one driver.

They were light, but strongly built. They had no

13. *This detail from a panel of one of the ceremonial chariots shows captive enemies of Egypt. The bonds ending in lily flowers show that the captive comes from the south; those ending in papyrus (center) show the captive is from the North.*

prings (which had not been invented), but the driver tood so far back that road shocks were absorbed partly by the pole, and the floor was a webbing which gave a certain amount of resilience. The six-spoked wheels were beautifully made—tough, light and springy; the tires were covered with leather. No seat was provided, and the vehicle was open at the back so that the driver could leap down quickly when necessary. Drawn by two powerful horses, the Egyptian chariot must have been a tricky thing to handle, especially at high speed, and even more difficult to shoot from. I imagine that the young King, whose sporting interests are obvious from other objects found in his tomb, was trained in both arts from an early age.

One of the most fascinating aspects of the whole discovery was the revelation, in the objects found, of ritual and religious formality combined with touches of simple humanity. Many of the treasures had been specially made to accompany Tutankhamen in the life beyond the tomb; others had clearly been things he had used and treasured in life—the great number of bows, for instance, and nearly three hundred arrows of differing types. Also he seems to have been a keen collector of sticks, some simple, some embellished with gold. There was one simple reed, the mounting of which bore the inscription: "A reed cut by His Majesty's own hand," and tucked under one of the couches was a tiny chair, too small to have been used by anyone but a child. There was also a sling with pebbles, and a number of games played with "men" on a squared surface.

Here was a sepulcher of the mighty Pharaoh, Lord of the Two Lands (Egypt was once two Kingdoms, the South and the North), son of Re the sun-god; a divine ruler who had been buried with pomp, with solemnity, and accompanied with immeasurable wealth, as befitted his royal power and divine nature. Yet it was also the tomb of a human boy with a boy's interests. There was evidence, too, of a personal tenderness standing out all the more vividly and movingly by contrast with the solemn splendor of the funerary equipment. There were simple floral wreaths leaning against the wall, perhaps placed there by the girl-queen, Ankhesenamun. Carter admits that at first it seemed a sacrilege to touch these tributes.

Gradually, methodically, with meticulous care, Carter, Callender, Mace, Lythgoe and the rest removed each precious artifact from the Antechamber, having first made certain that all future generations of archaeologists would have a complete pictorial record showing where each object had stood. The room was empty, all save the two guardian figures in black and gold, and a heap of sticks—probably arrows—which, together with a circular wicker basket, were piled against the lower part of the wall covering the breach made by the ancient tomb robbers. This heap of miscellaneous objects can be clearly seen in the photograph which Burton took to illustrate the cleared Antechamber.

At the risk of appearing to digress I would like to draw attention to this heap, which has long puzzled me. Carter states in his book that "close examination revealed the fact that a small breach had been made near the bottom, just wide enough to admit a boy or a slightly-built man, and that the hole had subsequently been filled up and re-sealed." Carter also published a photograph showing this resealed hole; in it the darker-colored plaster shows clearly where it had been refilled. (Fig. VI.) This plaster also bears the familiar seal of the Necropolis.

In the chapter describing preparations for opening the door Carter writes:

> By the middle of February our work in the Ante-chamber was finished. With the exception of the two sentinel statues, left for a special reason, all its contents had been removed to the laboratory, every inch of its floor had been swept and sifted for the last bead or fallen piece of inlay, and it now stood bare and empty.

In Burton's picture the couches have been removed; so has the painted casket which stood in front of the heap of arrows. Why, one asks, had they not also been removed when Carter's photograph was taken? Why were they left concealing the robbers' hole which, according to Burton's photograph had been blocked up and impressed with the seal of the Necropolis, exactly like those on the untouched part of the wall? Again, Carter's photograph shows that the resealed portion was distinctly darker than the rest. Would plaster have retained such a distinct contrast in coloration after three thousand years? It is curious, particularly as the other robbers' hole, between the Antechamber and the Annexe, had been left open. It is possible, of course, that the priests responsible for clearing up the tomb took the precaution of resealing the hole leading to the burial chamber, the most sacred part of the sepulcher, but the matter remains a mystery.

14. One of the three games of senet *included in the funerary chambers. It has not been possible to work out the rules of this game played by the Ancient Egyptians.*

On February 17, 1923, when an official party including Lord Carnarvon, Lady Evelyn Herbert, the Minister of Public Works, the Director-General of the Antiquities Service, and some twenty other personages attended the opening, the lower part of the wall was concealed behind a wooden platform built to enable Carter and his assistants to reach the topmost level of the sealed doorway when they began to demolish it. (See Fig. VII). The official party, seated on chairs in the now-empty Antechamber, watched while Carter began work, first searching for the wooden lintel above the door, and then slowly and painstakingly removing the stone filling, being careful to see that none of the blocks fell inward into the chamber beyond. Carter wrote, of this moment:

> . . . after about ten minutes I had made a hole large enough to enable me to . . . insert an electric torch. An astonishing sight it revealed, for there, within a yard of the doorway, stretching as far as one could see and blocking the entrance to the chamber, stood what to all appearance was a solid wall of gold. . . . We were at the entrance of the actual burial-chamber of the king, and that which barred our way was the side of an immense gilt shrine built to cover and protect the sarcophagus. It was visible now from the Antechamber by the light of the standard lamps, and as stone after stone was removed, and its gilded surface came gradually into

view, we could, as though by an electric current,
feel the tingle of excitement which thrilled the
spectators behind the barrier.[1]

The twenty or so human beings watching from the
Antechamber were to have an experience which no one
of our time, and probably no one in two thousand years,
has ever known: to be the first to enter the burial chamber
of a Pharaoh lying exactly as he was laid out three thousand years ago, surrounded by all his resplendent panoply
of death. One of them, Sir Alan Gardiner, gave me this
eyewitness account:

> We had seen such shrines depicted in ancient pa-
> pyri, but this was the real thing. There it was,
> splendid in its blue and gold, and almost filling the
> entire space of the second chamber. It reached
> nearly to the ceiling, and the space between it and
> the walls at the sides was not more than about two
> feet.
>
> First Carter and Carnarvon went in, squeezing
> their way through the narrow space, and we waited
> for them to return. When they came back they
> both lifted their hands in amazement at what they
> had seen. . . . When it came to my turn I went in
> with Professor Breasted. We pushed our way
> through and then turned left, so that we were op-

[1] Carter, Howard, and Mace, Arthur C., *The Tomb of Tut-Ankh-Amen*,
Vol. I. Cooper Square Publishers, Inc., New York, 1963.

15. Diagram showing the four golden shrines, the linen veil, the stone sarcophagus and the three mummiform coffins.

posite the front of the shrine, which had two great doors. Carter had drawn the bolt and opened these doors, so that we could see that inside the great outer shrine, which was 17 ft. long and 11 ft. wide, was another, smaller shrine, also with double doors, with the seal still unbroken. In fact there were in all four of these gilded shrines, one inside the other like a Chinese nest of boxes, and within the fourth was the sarcophagus and the coffins, which we were not to see until a year later. (See Fig. IX).

Sir Alan went on:

If you go to the Cairo Museum today you can see
these objects. They are still magnificent, of course,
but some of the gold has a slightly tarnished appearance. Now when we first entered the tomb the
gold shrines glittered with the greatest possible brilliancy. . . . Beyond the Burial Chamber we found
on the right the entrance to another room. . . . It
was full of marvels. There was the King's canopic
chest [containing the internal organs removed during embalmment] guarded by four delicate little
golden goddesses, two of whom were looking over
their shoulders towards us as if in protest at our
intrusion. There were more golden chariots, a great
shrouded effigy of the jackal-god Anubis, guardian
of the cemeteries; and there were many other
precious things, including a number of chests, boxes
and caskets. (See Figs. XVII, XVIII, XIX and
XXI). Carter opened one of these and on the top
lay a beautiful ostrich-feather fan. The feathers
were perfect, fluffing out just as if they had been
recently plucked, and waving gently in the slight
draught which came through the now-opened
doorway of the sepulchre. Those feathers completely annihilated the centuries for me. It was just
as if the King had been buried only a few days before. Of course in a few days they began to decay

and had to be preserved in paraffin wax, but when
I first saw them they were perfect; and they made
on me an impression such as I had never experienced before, and never shall again.[2]

*16. The god Anubis, of wood varnished black
with silver claws, eyes of alabaster and obsidian,
other details gilded.*

[2] From a BBC program by Leonard Cottrell called "The Tomb of
Tutankhamen" first broadcast 1947. Copyright by Mr. Cottrell.

Six

The Quarrel and the "Curse"

I have mentioned that Carter was not the least irritable of men, and he had to cope with problems which would have tried the nerves of any conscientious archaeologist. There was the unceasing stream of visitors sent by the Egyptian Government; there were the prying reporters gathered round the tomb entrance every day, resentful of the fact that only the correspondent of the London *Times* was allowed within the sepulcher during actual excavations. There was tension between Carter and Carnarvon themselves, for reasons which I have explained—mainly the fact that Carnarvon believed that, under the terms of the concession granted him by the Egyptian Government, a proportion of the finds belonged to him. With this Carter violently disagreed, saying that all the treasures were rightly the property of Egypt and should remain there.

In February, 1923, Carter quarrelled with his old friend and patron; there was an angry scene, after which, according to Charles Breasted, the son of the famous American archaeologist James Breasted, "Carter requested Car-

narvon to leave his house and never enter it again." Soon
after this Lord Carnarvon came down with fever brought
on by an infected insect-bite. Pneumonia set in, and on
April 5, 1923, Carnarvon died, at the age of fifty-seven.
Immediately the newspapers of the world sensationalized
this as "the Pharaoh's curse" and even went so far as to
say that Carnarvon had pricked his finger on some object
left deliberately in the tomb by its guardians.

The so-called "curse of Pharaoh" has become a
legend, and legends, once established, tend to stick. But
what are the facts? Ten years after the opening of the
tomb all but one of the five who first entered it were still
alive. Carter survived till 1939, dying at the age of sixty-
six. Burton, the photographer, and Rex Engelbach, Chief
Inspector of Antiquities, and later Director of the Cairo
Museum, also lived the normal span of years. Lady Evelyn
Herbert, now Lady Beauchamp, is, at the time of writing,
still alive. Dr. Derry, who performed the dissection of the
Pharaoh's mummy (and should therefore be especially ac-

17. *Among the most elaborate containers, possibly for perfume, found in the Annexe is the
alabaster boat. The ibex on the figurehead has
real horns; the young girl holds a lotus flower.
The alabaster is inlaid with colored glass-paste
and decorated with semi-precious stones and
gold leaf.*

cursed) lived to be over eighty. Sir Alan Gardiner died in December, 1963, in his mid-eighties.

In fact the "curse" is pure nonsense, and should be regarded as such. But the legend is now so well established that even in 1954, when I had contracted dengue fever in Egypt and, as a result, developed a lame knee for a few weeks, an English newspaper came out with the headline: "BBC Producer and Author Cursed by the Pharaoh" (because I happened to mention to a journalist friend that I had spent some time watching the excavation of a Pharaonic pyramid!).

People who heed such fanciful stuff must have starved imaginations. The real facts about Tutankhamen's tomb are much more romantic than any fiction. For instance, let us look at the real story of what happened after the opening of the Second Chamber containing the great gilded shrines and the three coffins. During the season 1923 to 1924, work was concentrated on dismantling and removing the four golden shrines which occupied almost the entire space of the burial chamber. This was a task which taxed Carter's ingenuity to the utmost, but in the end the shrines were taken apart without damage and removed to Cairo. On February 14, 1924, in the presence of leading officials, the lid of the quartzite sarcophagus, which lay within the innermost shrine, was raised, and the onlookers saw for the first time the splendid outer coffin of the Pharaoh, of wood plated with gold and inlaid with semi-precious stones.

And on the very same day the following notice appeared in the principal hotels in Luxor:

Owing to the impossible restriction and discourtesies on the part of the Public Works Department and its Antiquities Service, all my collaborators in protest have refused to work any further upon the scientific investigation of the discovery of the Tomb of Tutankhamun. I am therefore obliged to make known to the public that immediately after the Press view of the tomb this morning between 10:00 A.M. and noon the tomb will be closed and no further work carried out.

(Signed) HOWARD CARTER

This was the culmination of Carter's dispute with the Egyptian Government. The crux of his complaints was that by harassing him with minute instructions as to the manner in which he conducted the work, and by sending him streams of visitors, the Government had made it impossible for him to carry out his delicate and exacting task. In this he was fully supported by his colleagues, American and British. One of them, Breasted, wrote:

The scientific men agreed that, however injudicious and temperamental his behaviour had been at times ... the Egyptian Government's treatment had been so inconsiderate as to have forced remonstrative action upon him.[1]

The effect of this announcement was immediate. The Government took over the tomb, reopened it to visitors,

[1] Breasted, Charles, *Pioneer to the Past*. Charles Scribner's Sons, New York, 1943.

and invited large numbers of officials and their wives to see it. A British journalist who watched these proceedings, which were rounded off by fireworks, commented at the time:

> A pathetic note was provided by two of Mr. Carter's trusted Egyptian foremen, faithfully guarding a heap of their master's property, not far from the mouth of the tomb for the discovery of which they had served him with such unflagging fidelity and perseverance. Their saddened faces left no doubt as to their thoughts at seeing the careless throng passing into the tomb which, to them and their master, represented the almost sacred crowning of the labour of a lifetime.[2]

It is worth noticing here that the workmen were almost certainly "Qufti," that is from the village of Quft in Upper Egypt. The distinguished British excavator Sir Flinders Petrie had recruited most of his workmen from this village before Carter's time, and even to this day the best and most reliable Egyptian workmen, trained for archaeological "digs," usually come from this village. When I was watching the late Zakaria Goneim excavating a buried pyramid in 1954, his *reis* or foremen were Qufts; and that was in 1954.

In his book *The Tomb of Tut-ankh-amen* Carter reprints a moving letter in imperfect English from his head man or *reis*, sent to him at the time when he was prevented

[2] *Egyptian Gazette*, March, 1924.

by officialdom from re-entering the tomb. It is well worth reprinting here, since it provides such a striking contrast between the loyalty and affection of the trained Egyptian archaeological helper, who has probably spent his life (from the days when he was a mere "basket-boy," carrying debris in baskets) in helping European and American excavators do their scientific work, and the minor government officials who, like most government officials everywhere, are overconcerned with rules and regulations. The letter reads:

> *Honourable Sir,*
>   Beg to write this letter hoping you are enjoying good health, and ask the Almighty to keep you and bring you back to us in safety. Beg to inform you that Store No. 15 is alright, Treasure is alright, the Northern Store is alright, Wadain and House is alright, and in all your work order is carried on according to your honourable instructions. Reis Hussein, Gad Hassan, Hassan Awad Abdelal Ahmed and all the *ghaffirs* [guardians] of the house beg to send their best regards.
>   *My best regards to your honourable self.*
>   *Longing to your early coming,*
>   *Your obedient servant,*
>   REIS AHMED GURGAR*³*

It is more than probable that Carter would never have been allowed to return to the tomb but for the tragedy

---

³ Carter and Mace, *op. cit.*

of the assassination of a senior British Officer, Sir Lee Stack, in November, 1924. In the meantime Carter had fought a lawsuit with the Egyptian Government but without success. But from the moment the killer shot Sir Lee Stack on the doorstep of his home in Cairo, such was the anger aroused in British Government circles that the British, who had up to that time been relinquishing their hold on Egyptian affairs, re-established firm control. As an indirect result the legal conflicts concerning the Tomb of Tutankhamen were forgotten, and Carter was allowed to return.

Reis Ahmed Gurgar, Reis Hussein, Gad Hassan, Hassan Awad Abdelal Ahmed and the rest of his faithful *ghaffirs* were waiting when their master returned. The iron grille swung open, and once again Carter was in the presence of the dead Pharaoh, still lying in the innermost of the three coffins, the outer of which could be seen under the plate glass screen which Carter had placed there for its protection. The footsteps of the great archaeologist and his helpers echoed in the rock-cut chamber. Of this moment Carter wrote in his book:

> Once more we entered the Burial Chamber. Once more our powerful electric lamps lit up the great quartzite sarcophagus. Under the plate-glass screen . . . was revealed the gold-encased outer coffin that

18. *A sacred cow, one of the forms of the god-dess Hathor. The head is of gilded and stuccoed wood; the eyes are of crystalline limestone and obsidian, outlined with black glass, which also forms the eyebrows. The horns are wood which has been plated with bronze leaf.*

seems to gather power of appealing to the emotions
the moment it is seen. With the shadows of the ancient gods there can be no vulgar intimacy. . . .[4]

But there was one bitter moment for Carter. When the
burial chamber had first been disclosed a delicate linen
pall had been found draped over the inner shrine (the one
which enclosed the outermost of the three coffins). Carter
had had to remove it in order to dismantle the shrine and
get at the sarcophagus. But in his absence the Egyptian
officials, instead of replacing the pall within the tomb,
where it would have been safe, had left it exposed to the
fierce summer sun in an improvised shed or shelter outside.
When Carter returned, all that remained of this unique
piece of three-thousand-year-old fabric were a few rap-
idly decaying fragments. A newspaper commentator of
the time wrote:

> Mr. Carter's agitation was intense, but he contented
> himself with one remark:
> "Well, anyway, it was your Pall, not mine . . .
> and it *was* the only one in the world."

---

[4] Carter and Mace, *op cit*.

Seven

The Three Coffins

I t may be helpful at this stage to remember what Sir
Alan Gardiner, one of the fortunate few who were
privileged to enter the burial chamber at its first opening,
said about it:

*We had seen such things in ancient papyri, but here
was the real thing.*

The Ancient Egyptians were fond of depicting, on the
walls of their tombs, especially the tombs of nonroyal personages, scenes familiar to them in their everyday life. For
instance in the tomb of a great official named Rekhmire, at
Thebes, there is a scene showing workmen making what
we call "funerary equipment" that is, shrines, statuary and
the like intended for a royal burial. Rekhmire happened
to be Superintendent of the Royal Workshops of the God
Amun, and in the tomb paintings he is shown overseeing
the labors of his workmen, some of whom are making caskets, vases, and even a statue of King Tuthmosis III (one

of Tutankhamen's predecessors) for the approval of their master. That is what Sir Alan meant by "We had seen such things"—not only in ancient papyri (which were his particular study) but on the walls of tombs. The discovery of Tutankhamen's sepulcher, enthralling though it was, did not have such elements of the *unknown* as excited the world when Heinrich Schliemann discovered the graves of hitherto-unknown kings and queens at Mycenae in Greece, or when Sir Arthur Evans, in 1899, came upon the remains of a great Palace at Knossos in Crete dating from before 2000 B.C. There were no written or pictorial records of such places, whereas in Ancient Egypt there were.

But, until Carter found the burial of Tutankhamen, no human being had ever set eyes on the royal coffins of a Pharaoh, intact, undisturbed by robbers, standing within the nest of gold-encased wooden shrines as they had been placed in the narrow chamber more than thirty centuries ago. You may be surprised by the word "coffins" in the plural. Why more than one coffin? We do not know, except that there may have been some religious meaning in the actual *number* of protective devices surrounding the body of the King, who was also a God.

Dr. Margaret Murray, the distinguished archaeologist and anthropologist who died in 1963 at the age of one hundred years, once pointed out to me that, to the ancient peoples, seven was a "lucky number." There were *four* outer shrines protecting the coffins, and *three* inner coffins, each nesting within the other; seven in all. Whether this was coincidental or deliberate we shall probably never know.

So Carter began the last stage of his task, the opening of the three coffins, each enclosed within the next like a Chinese nest of boxes. The opening of these coffins taxed all Carter's resourcefulness. They nested within each other so tightly, he tells us, that it was not possible to pass one's little finger between them. Moreover the funeral libations poured over them at the time of interment had solidified like cement. The problem was to remove the inner coffins without damaging the delicate inlay of carnelian and lapis-lazuli, set within tiny semicircles of gold which shimmered like the scales of a fish. Of these tense weeks Carter wrote:

> Everything may seem to be going well when suddenly you hear a crack. Little pieces of surface ornament fall. Your nerves are at an almost painful tension. What is happening? All available room in the narrow space is crowded with your men. What is needed to avert a catastrophe? They all look at you. *You* must find the answer.[1]

Thanks to Carter's patience and engineering skill all these problems were overcome. The second and third (inner) coffins were removed from the large outer one

[1] Carter and Mace, *op. cit.*

with all their blazonry of gold leaf, carnelian and lapis. Each was of "anthropoid" shape, *i.e.*, in the form of a mummified human body, and each had on its lid a representation of the boy king, his arms crossed upon his breast and carrying the twin insignia of Ancient Egyptian royalty, the crook and the flail. And on each coffin was represented the head of the Pharaoh wearing the "false beard," the wig and royal headdress surmounted by two more symbols on the brow: the cobra or uraeus, representing Lower Egypt, and the vulture, representing dominion over Upper Egypt. (See illustration on page 103.)

Such symbols of majesty had been worn on the crown of the Pharaohs for more than one thousand years before Tutankhamen was born, and were a memory of the far-distant period, before 3000 B.C., when Egypt was divided into two Kingdoms, the North and the South.

Within the second coffin lay the third and last, and this,

19. The second coffin, made of compact wood covered with sheets of gold inlaid with multi-colored glass paste and semi-precious stones. It shows the mummified figure of the god Osiris holding his insignia in his crossed arms and wearing the long beard of the gods. The coffin is 6 feet, 8 inches long.

when revealed, filled the discoverers with awe. For it was of solid gold, so heavy that it needed four men to lift it. The lid represented the Pharaoh in all his splendid regalia. The face was a portrait; below it his crossed arms held, again, the sacred crook and flail. The goldwork was the masterpiece of a craftsman of genius. Inlaid within the shining metal was a shimmering pattern of carnelian and lapis, each tiny stone inset with the utmost care. (See Figs. XI, XII, and XIII).

Below the crossed arms, incised on the gold, were representations of two lovely goddesses, each with wings which enfolded the body of the young Pharaoh, as if to protect him. The discoverers gazed, astonished, at this revelation, and it seemed to Carter, as he says in his book, that "we

20. The finest gold funerary mask ever found anywhere in the world, and probably the best portrait in gold ever made. It is doubtless an exact likeness of young Tutankhamen and is life-size. Semi-precious stones inlay the beaten gold and lapis-lazuli makes up the eyes and eyebrows. The false beard of the gods adorns the young sovereign's chin. The height of the mask is 21 inches.

were in the presence of the dead King, and must do him reverence." It is not easy to imagine the mixed feelings of those privileged to make this discovery. They had stumbled upon the intact burial of a Pharaoh, the only one ever found in his original coffin and tomb. The priests of those far-off times, long before Greece or Rome had been conceived, or half the recorded history of mankind had been written, had taken fantastic precautions to guard and protect the royal body, even though, as we shall see, Tutankhamen was only a minor king, almost the last of a declining and unpopular dynasty.

And here stood the scientific excavators of the twentieth century, torn between respect and awe for the long-dead King, and curiosity about the body which lay within the golden inner coffin. Was the body well preserved, like that of Sethos I and Ramesses III? Would it be possible, once the mummy wrappings were removed, to look on the actual features of Tutankhamen? There could be no doubt concerning the outcome. The second and inner coffins were carried from the tomb to that of Sethos I, which served Carter and his colleagues as a laboratory, the lid was removed, and the final work of unwrapping was begun. The surgeon and anatomist, Dr. Derry, stood by to perform an autopsy or "post-mortem" on the royal corpse, just as if it was a body of recent date, and not that of the ruler of Egypt more than three thousand years ago. Science is remorseless.

Eight

The Pharaoh Is Revealed

The lid of the gold coffin was secured to its base by tongues sliding into grooves. When the archaeologists removed the lid, in the brilliant electric light installed in Sethos's tomb, there lay before them the elaborately wrapped mummy of the Pharaoh and the most wonderful sight of all, a golden portrait head of the young monarch, inlaid with blue lapis and wearing the royal cobra and vulture on its brow, as on the outer coffin. (See Fig. XIV). From the drawing on page 104 you can get some idea of this superb example of the Ancient Egyptian goldsmith's art by some unknown artist who is worthy to stand beside Cellini and any of the finest goldsmiths of the Renaissance.

Having recovered from their astonishment, the next problem facing the archaeologists was that of removing the mummy from under the mask, and this proved extremely difficult, as, when the body had been laid in the coffin more than three thousand years ago, funeral libations had been poured over it and these, solidifying, had attached the mask to the coffin, as firmly as strong glue. Not only that, but the same libations (Carter estimated that two bucketfuls of liquid had been poured in) had caused the inner, gold coffin to adhere to the second, wooden coffin.

Here indeed was a problem; how to separate the two coffins and remove the gold mask. The excavators first tried exposing them to the fierce Egyptian sun, but to no effect. Carter's final solution, a masterpiece of ingenuity, will be studied later. Meanwhile Dr. Douglas Derry, the surgeon and anatomist, set about unwrapping the mummy, removing it from under the gold mask, and then examining the bones. In his own words, which he recorded for me in 1949:

> Over the head and shoulders, reaching down to the middle of the body, was a solid gold mask representing an effigy of the young king. . . . This mask was firmly stuck to the floor of the coffin by certain resinated materials . . . the mummy was glued to the floor and it was some days before I was able to release the body and draw the head and shoulders out of the mask which remained stuck to the bottom of the coffin by the rock-like hardness of the dried resins. . . . As the one who actually unwrapped the mummy of the King the supposed curse should rest most heavily on me, and I should, have been the first to die. But I've survived it 26 years and I am now 74.

Actually Dr. Derry lived on into his eighties.

As each layer of mummy wrappings was removed it was seen that the Pharaoh's body was bedizened with more gold and jewelry. Necklaces of gold and semiprecious stones encircled his neck; his fingers gleamed with gold rings; even his fingernails and toenails were fitted with tiny gold sheaths. Around his slender body were trappings of heavy gold plaques bearing welcoming speeches by gods and goddesses addressed to the young King—he was probably about seventeen or eighteen when he died—as he entered the Underworld to join his fellow deities. According to Egyptian belief the Pharaoh was the son of Re, god of the sun, and would, on his death, join the gods.

These greetings are extremely moving and beautiful. The goddess Nut (pronounced Newt) thus addresses him:

> *I reckon thy beauties, O Osiris, King Kheperu-Neb-Re; thy soul liveth; thy veins are firm. Thou smellest the air and goeth out as a God, going out as Atum, O Osiris, Tutankhamun. . . .*

And Geb, god of the Earth, says to him:

> *My beloved son, inheritor of the throne of Osiris, the King Kheperu-Neb-Re; thy nobility is perfect; thy Royal Palace is powerful; . . . thy stability is in the mouth of the living; O Osiris, Tutankhamun. . . .*

What was the meaning of these inscriptions, of which there were several others? They were magical spells which were believed to assure the King's immortality. Osiris was the Egyptian God of the Dead and Judge of Souls, originally, but after a time every king (and indeed everyone who could afford a tomb) became *"an* Osiris" followed by his name. Incidentally Kheperu-Neb-Re (or in some readings Neb-Kheperu-Re) was one of the royal names, of which Tutankhamen was another. Notice particularly the emphasis on the physical preservation of the body . . . "thy veins are firm" etc. In another text occur the words, "Thy heart is in thy body eternally" (very important, because to the Ancient Egyptians the heart, not the brain, was the center of intelligence and feeling).

When the pathetic little body was finally revealed, it proved to be that of a mere boy in his late 'teens; the skull was not as well preserved as that of some royal mummies, but sufficient remained to satisfy the anatomist that the unknown genius who made the golden mask had faithfully portrayed the features of the dead Pharaoh. (See Figs. XV and XVI). The cause of his early death remains unknown.

The next problem was the removal of the sumptuous solid-gold coffin from the inner, wooden one, in such a way as not to damage either. Carter eventually decided to line the interior of the gold coffin with zinc plates, and then, supporting the two coffins, on trestles, upside down,

21. This head of the child-king was found at the
entry of the tomb, set upon a pedestal in the
shape of a lotus flower. It is of stuccoed and
painted wood.

over several paraffin stoves, he succeeded in melting the resins so that the two could be separated. But it was a tricky operation. The outside, wooden coffin was covered with blankets saturated with water, and Carter had to regulate the temperature of the paraffin stoves so that the heat never approached the melting point of zinc (520 degrees Centigrade, 968 degrees Farenheit).

Finally the first, or outer wooden coffin, which had been left within the sarcophagus, was lifted out by hoisting tackle slung from overhead scaffolding. This too, was accomplished without damage to the coffin, which now stands in the Egyptian Museum in Cairo, together with the inner, golden coffin and the mask. When all the work was over, the body of the King was laid reverently in its second coffin and replaced within the sarcophagus in the tomb, where it still lies today.

Nine

Romance and Reality

There are in this fantastic story elements of high romance and earthy reality. It is almost heartbreaking—the contrast between the splendor of the God-King, surrounded by all his panoply of wealth and power, walking into the sunlight of immortality, welcomed by his fellow gods, and the huddle of bones within the mummy wrappings being scientifically examined by an anatomist. Surely no two worlds could seem more opposite in character than our own and that of Ancient Egypt. The elaborate precautions taken by the Egyptians to protect the body of their monarch, the custom of burying with him such riches as truly befit the words "a King's ransom"; the belief in magical spells and the efficacy of paintings and sculpture, not as objects of art, but as tokens of one's wealth and an assurance that one would continue to enjoy in the next world all that one had enjoyed in this one—contrast all this with our own comparative indifference to the fate of our earthly bodies, our reliance not on magical spells but on scientifically established fact. What a difference!

And yet, in many ways the Ancient Egyptians, for all their (to us) strange beliefs, were very like us. Take the objects found in Tutankhamen's Tomb. Among the golden splendor were ordinary human things: a child's games and toys; a "keepsake" in the form of a lock of hair from the head of Queen Tiye. Again there is the clear evidence of tenderness and affection between the young king and his queen Ankhesenamun, both little more than children, as we see on the relief which adorns the back of the Throne. Among the golden regalia were the bodies of two stillborn children, each in its little coffin, evidence that Ankhesenamun had twice tried to bear a child. Probably —almost certainly in fact—she was left a childless widow, which has important bearing on the story we shall tell in the last chapter of this book.

Coming to our own scientific world, we have nothing at which we need feel ashamed concerning the excavation of Tutankhamen's burial, except for the vulgar and unnecessary disputes which accompanied it, and which might have brought the whole operation into jeopardy. If the tomb had been discovered by the ordinary Egyptian "illicit-digger" or tomb robber, certainly a few of the more valuable objects would have come onto the market, but many would have been destroyed for the sake of the gold,

22. Model of the pharaoh's boat which could have taken him on his trips up or down the Nile.

and much valuable historical information would have been lost forever, as it was in the case of all the other royal burials.

As it happened, thanks to the determination, skill and perseverance of Carter and Lord Carnarvon, this unique discovery—and there is unlikely ever to be another one—was carried out under the strictest scientific control. Experts from Britain and the United States readily gave their services, and the result is that nowadays every visitor to Cairo can wander through a suite of galleries containing all the objects found in the tomb, displayed in full splendor and adequately protected against decay.

Two men in particular should be commended for this: one is the late Rex Engelbach, an Englishman, formerly Director of the Museum, who was mainly responsible for arranging and displaying the objects; the other is A. Lucas, a chemist and one-time scientific adviser to the Museum, who was responsible for the measures which succeeded in preserving the more fragile objects.

There were also the distinguished American experts such as Lythgoe, Curator of the Egyptian Department of the Metropolitan Museum of Art, New York; Burton, their photographic expert; Winlock and Mace, also of the New York Metropolitan Museum, and others. The late Dr. Derry did the autopsy on the mummy; Sir Alan Gardiner, recently deceased, came out specially to help decipher the inscriptions; the late Professor Percy Newberry gave his services as botanist and identified the wreaths and other floral tributes found in the tomb.

Of these men, three were known personally to me, and as death removes, one by one, the little band who first entered the tomb, it is something to have spoken to a few and heard their story firsthand.

I remember Mrs. Newberry, who died shortly after her

husband, telling me about the wonderful linen pall which was found draped over the inner shrine. The most remarkable thing about it, she said, was that the hemming and stitching had been done in exactly the same way it would have been done today. It was Mrs. Newberry who carefully rethreaded all the delicate jeweled necklaces now on view at the Museum in Cairo. The original thread had of course perished. Carter had the beads photographed exactly as they lay and then Mrs. Newberry rethreaded them. "Some of the beads," she remarked "were so tiny

23. The king's two daggers. The blade of the top dagger is of gold, as is the sheath above it decorated with animals. The blade of the other dagger is of iron with a rock crystal knob on the handle; its sheath is also of gold.

that it would have been impossible to see the holes but for the wonderful Egyptian sunlight."

Newberry himself told me that one of the floral wreaths, placed near the sealed door of the sepulcher, could, perhaps, have been laid there by Queen Ankhesenamun herself.

When you go to Cairo today, and enter the Museum, you may at first be slightly disappointed. The gold, after more than forty years, has a slightly tarnished appearance, as mentioned earlier. But Sir Alan Gardiner told me that when he first saw it, it shone with extraordinary brilliancy, as if it had been left there yesterday, and not more than three thousand years ago.

Today one is likely to be hustled through the Museum by dragomans (guides) along with many other tourists, and it is not always easy to recapture in one's imagination that awesome moment when Carter peered through a hole in the outer, sealed door and, with eyes growing accustomed to the light, saw everywhere the gleam of gold. . . . Of all the human beings who have lived during the last troubled half-century, the one I envy most is Carter, the first human being to see the full glory of a Pharaoh's treasure after it had lain in darkness for over thirty centuries.

Ten

Why Did it Happen?

One important question remains to be answered. Why was it that, alone among more than thirty Pharaonic tombs in the Royal Valley, that of Tutankhamen survived down to the twentieth century? Much of the credit is obviously due to the patience and persistence of Howard Carter who, even when his patron was on the point of giving up excavating in the Valley, persuaded him to finance one more season's digging, on the grounds that there was one small triangular area, near the tomb of Ramesses VI, which had not been thoroughly investigated.

But there is more to it than that. All the other tombs of Kings had been looted in remote antiquity. Why had that of Tutankhamen been spared, or overlooked? One could answer that it was a very small sepulcher compared with those of such mighty kings as Sethos I and Ramesses II. But practically all the tombs of the nobles or high officials, situated on the eastern side of the Theban cliffs, had been systematically robbed thousands of years ago, and they were usually even smaller than that of Tutankhamen.

No, there must be some other explanation, or maybe several explanations. In my opinion the clue lies in the fact that Tutankhamen was a near relative of the so-called Heretic King Amenophis IV, who renamed himself Akhenaten which means, "It is well with the Aten." The "Aten" was Akhenaten's god, a solar disk with descending rays which he intended should replace all the many deities of Egypt as the One God all men should worship. In particular he detested Amun-Re, King of Gods, whose worship was centered at Thebes and for this reason the idealistic Pharaoh removed his capital to a virgin site midway between Thebes and modern Cairo. There you may still see the ruins of his short-lived city called Tell el Amarna, and the tombs of his great officials cut out of the rocky cliffs to the east. In all of these you see the symbol of the One God, the "Aten" just as you see it on the backrest of Tutankhamen's throne (see page 55).

Akhenaten's queen was the lovely Nefertiti, whose famous portrait bust, found by German excavators at Tell el Amarna is perhaps the best-known of all Egyptian sculptured heads. Tutankhamen, originally called Tutankh-*aten*, may have been her son, or at least the son of her husband by one of his other wives (for in Ancient Egypt it was permissible for a King to have several wives, besides concubines). Certainly he was brought up by her in his early youth, and there can be little doubt that some of the furniture found in his tomb came originally from the

Royal Palace of Akhenaten, where Tutankhamen's girl-queen, Ankhesenamun, was also educated in the Aten-faith. Her name was originally *Ankhesenpaaten.*

When Akhenaten died, the Court moved back to Thebes; in fact it seems possible that toward the end of his reign Akhenaten was seeking a compromise with the priests of the older god Amun, at Thebes, and sent one of his sons, Smenkhkare, there, later to be joined by Tutankhaten (as he was still named) and his wife. One theory is that it was Nefertiti and not Akhenaten who was the most devoted "Atenist" and that she nurtured Tutankhaten while her husband lavished his affection on Smenkhkare, who was either Tutankhaten's brother or half-brother.

The whole period is obscure; no one can be certain what happened during the declining years of the Eighteenth Dynasty (1400–1350 B.C.). The general impression is of royal children being used in a political power game between ambitious politicians such as General Horemheb and an elder statesman named Ay or Eye. Both subsequently became Pharaohs in the usual way, by marrying the royal heiresses. This was the way power passed from a Pharaoh to his successor. To become a Pharaoh you had to marry the widow or daughter of your predecessor. It was probably for this reason that brothers married sisters (or half-sisters), so that the power of succession should remain within the royal family.

What we do know for certain is that the young Tutankhaten changed his name to Tutankh*amen*, and Ankhesenpaaten to Ankhesen*amun*, each incorporating into his
or her name that of the old god of Thebes, Amun. Thus
Amun triumphed, and after the death of the hated heretic
Akhenaten the old religion was re-established at Thebes.
The Heretic King was vilified; his name was erased from
his monuments and his capital destroyed.

Now imagine the situation of the young Tutankhamen
and his wife at such a period. They were little more than
children, given due reverence as king and queen, yet
knowing all the time that they were surrounded by ambitious, scheming older people, anxious to obtain power
by any means. Despite the fact that they had, officially,
abandoned the New Religion and embraced the older
faith, they still were members of an unpopular Dynasty.
Moreover, as we know that Akhenaten suffered from a
disease which caused malformation of the skull and limbs,
it is more than likely that Tutankhamen also was in poor
health. Generations of inbreeding, brother-and-sister mar-
riages, had weakened the royal stock. It was very near its
end.

Funerary furniture was made during their brief young
lives to acompany the royal bodies on the journey to the
world beyond the grave. Such furniture—gilded shrines,
coffins, couches, caskets etc.—was kept in the storerooms
of Amun for eventual use. But it is a curious fact that,

24. *Detail from the lid of an ivory-inlaid chest.*
Tutankhamen and Ankhesenamum are shown,
probably at the beginning of their reign. The
queen is offering the king a bunch of lotus and
papyrus flowers. Both wear pleated linen with
long, flowing sashes.

among the objects found in the tomb of Tutankhamen there were some (*e.g.*, the shrines) which had originally been meant for his half-brother (or brother) Smenkhkare. One can see where the royal cartouche (the name of the Pharaoh surrounded by a flattened oval) has been altered.

Smenkhkare, who preceded Tutankhamen as Pharaoh, reigned for only a few years, and some authorities believe that the body of the young man found in the so-called "Tomb of Tiye" (Akhenaten's mother) is that of the young Pharaoh. Others have recently advanced the theory that the body is that of the Heretic King, Akhenaten himself, pointing out that the disease from which he suffered would have had the effect of preventing the bones from attaining their normal growth, so that, though the body appears to be that of a young man, it could be that of a man of forty. Again, we do not know. It is a mystery.

But to return to the Tomb of Tutankhamen and the reason why it remained intact for three thousand years. Everything points to the fact that the tomb was *not* originally intended for a Pharaoh. First, it is very small compared with those of such Kings as Tuthmosis III, Amenophis II, Ramesses II and Sethos I. It could, possibly, have been intended for the burial of a privileged nobleman, perhaps related to the Royal Family, a man who was permitted the rare honor of being buried in the Royal Valley.

The tomb of Yuya and Thuya, discovered by Theodore Davis in 1903, springs to mind.

Now the principal celebrant depicted on the wall paintings in Tutankhamen's burial chamber is the politician Ay (or Eye) who had been one of Akhenaten's closest advisers (he had another tomb prepared at Tell el Amarna) and who subsequently married Tutankhamen's widow, Ankhesenamun, and thus made himself Pharaoh. It is tempting to think that this little, insignificant sepulcher was built for Ay, and that when he became Pharaoh, on the death of Tutankhamen, he buried the boy king in the small tomb he had made for himself, while he prepared a much larger tomb to contain his own body when he died. His own tomb exists, not far from that of Amenophis III in the Western Valley, though it is not normally accessible to the public.

This would explain why the relatively minor tomb of Tutankhamen was stuffed with treasure obviously designed for a much larger burial place (remember that the outermost of the four golden shrines within the burial chamber almost touched the walls and ceiling). The Antechamber and Annexe were crowded to the ceiling with marvels, and the royal chariots had had to be sawed in pieces to admit them to the narrow chamber. One may well imagine the rich Ancient Egyptian curses of the workmen who, by royal decree, were forced to assemble three royal coffins, a sarcophagus, and four wooden shrines within less than half the space which they had been intended to occupy. No wonder they put the shrines in the wrong way round, as Carter discovered!

There is no written record of this. We can only deduce the probable facts from the material evidence, like a detective following up clues. Then what happened? Clearly the position of the tomb was well known to the ancient tomb robbers, who, as we have seen, entered it more than once, but were unable to steal more than a few easily portable objects. Evidently they entered the burial chamber—the hole at the bottom of the sealed doorway proves that—but again were able only to take away a few small things. The Pharaoh's burial remained inviolate.

Clearly the guardians of the royal cemetery were, at this time, exceptionally vigilant, since they were able to prevent the thieves removing more than a few articles, and at one stage interrupted a robbery, so that one of the plunderers was forced to leave on the floor the few golden rings he had hurriedly knotted in a piece of linen (unless the thief was caught red-handed and the loot subsequently returned to the tomb).

Before resealing the entrance for what proved to be the last time for three thousand years, the priests of the Necropolis hurriedly "tidied up" the tomb, but did not bother to restore the objects to their original caskets or boxes. Hence the scene of confusion which greeted Carter and Carnarvon when they first entered the sepulcher; hence the chaotic state of the Annexe, glimpsed through a tomb-robber's hole in the wall, wherein lay all kinds of precious things hurled higgledy-piggledy where the

25. An ivory headrest, stained dark green, red-brown and black.

thieves had left them, even to the footprint of one of the would-be robbers clearly showing on a bow case.

But what happened to the girl-queen, Ankhesenamun? No one knows, except that, in the end, she married Ay, a man in his sixties. There is, however, a fascinating piece of correspondence preserved in the archives of the royal capital of the Hittites at Hattusas (Boghaz-koy) in modern Turkey. The Hittites were a powerful people, ruled by kings reigning in the highlands of Asia Minor. From time to time they came into conflict with the Ancient Egyptians in Syria; the Egyptians, on their monuments, described these enemies as "the abominable *Kheta*" (Hati or Hittites) though in later years the two empires became allies.

Some sixty-odd years ago a German archaeologist named Winckler excavated Hattusas and found a large number of baked-clay tablets inscribed in the ancient Babylonian cuneiform (wedge-shaped) writing. Among these royal archives was a series of letters from an unknown Egyptian queen addressed to the Hittite King Suppiluliuma, who is known to have led his armies to the borders of Egypt's Syrian colonies round about the time of Tutankahmen's reign. The dates are not precise, but near enough.

Among these tablets (having no paper the Hittites used

baked clay for their correspondence) are letters addressed to Suppiluliuma. The first reads:

> *My husband has died and I have no son, but of you it is said that you have many sons. If you would send one of your sons, he could become my husband. I will on no account take one of my subjects and make him my husband. I am very much afraid. . . .*

"I am very much afraid." This does not sound like a letter from a mature, experienced stateswoman, but from a frightened young girl.

Still, we do not know who the unknown queen was as one cannot be certain of the precise dates. A later letter, found in the same collection at Hattusas, is evidently written in reply to one from King Suppiluliuma which has been lost. From its content one assumes that the cautious Hittite monarch had doubted the truth of the Egyptian queen's earlier message. She replies, in some anger:

> *Why do you say, "They are deceiving me"? If I had a son, would I write to a foreigner [observe the note of contempt] to publish my distress and that of my country? You have insulted me by speaking thus. . . . My husband is dead and I have no son. I will never take one of my subjects and marry him.*

I have written to no-one but you. Everyone says
you have many sons; give me one of them that he
may become my husband.

Good archaeologists like Carter are cautious people.
They deal, not with written documents of known date,
as historians do, but with tangible objects which can sometimes be dated. Occasionally written records turn up, as
in this case, but again it is necessary to be careful in
ascribing them to any particular person unless they are
signed. In another letter from these Hittite archives the
name of the dead Egyptian king is rendered as "Dahk-
amun" which *could* be Tutankhamen. However, it is
permissible to speculate and form deductions, as a good
detective does, and every known fact points to the unknown queen being Ankhesenamun, Tutankhamen's widow, who was probably not more than sixteen when those
letters were written.

Why can we assume this to be true? First, because the
dates fit. Second, because we know for certain that royal
inheritance in Ancient Egypt was *always through the*
female line. Whoever married the heiress of a Pharaoh,
whether his widow or daughter (if the wife was dead)
could become Pharaoh and rule Egypt. Third, we know
from the presence of the stillborn children in Tutankhamen's tomb that his girl-wife had attempted to bear him
children but they had died. If any of her children by

Tutankhamen had survived, there would almost certainly have been some record of them. Fourth, we know that Ay, who had held high rank under Akhenaten, subsequently married Ankhesenamun and became Pharaoh. These facts are on record.

What we do *not* know is what happened during the period of about one hundred days during which the Pharaoh's dead body was soaking in its bath of natron (a preservative fluid) and preparations were being made for its

26. *The scribe's ivory palette (above) bears Tutankhamen's names and describes him as "beloved of the gods." Two cakes of red and blue-black ink still remain in their containers and in the central hollow seven reeds were found. The case for holding the writing reeds (top) is gilded wood inlaid with semi-precious stones. The cap is of ivory, held in place by a catch.*

burial. Ay was over sixty; Ankhesenamun was probably not more than sixteen or seventeen. Would she wish to marry Ay? It seems highly unlikely. But, surrounded as she was by suave courtiers and ambitious, smooth-tongued statesmen, and knowing, as she must have, that during the brief period before her dead husband was buried no one could *compel* her to marry, what would be more natural than that she should stretch out her hand in desperation to the Hittite King, who, as she wrote (if it was Ankhesenamun who wrote those letters) "had many sons"?

It was her last chance. She was very young, probably beautiful, and, as she admits in one of her letters "very much afraid." My own belief is that if, indeed, Ankhesenamun wrote those pathetic letters, in which royal pride mingles with pleading, she was one of the bravest women of history. To get those letters to the Hittite King at all, without detection, was an act of great diplomatic subtlety and skill. Again, she had to risk the snubs she might (and indeed did) receive. But when she writes, defiantly *"I will*

27. The front part of an unguent jar which shows an ibex, crouching and bleating. The horns were real, the one on the right drawn in by the artist. The eyes have been inlaid with bronze and glass-paste and the ivory tongue is stained red. The royal cartouche is dark blue.

*on no account take one of my subjects and make him my
husband*" I am certain that she is thinking only of one
"subject," the ambitious, sixty-year-old politician Ay.

Alas, her gamble failed. Whether or not the Hittite
King sent one of his sons, we know that in the end
Tutankhamen was ceremonially buried; Ay performed
the funerary rites, wearing the sacred leopard skin, as you
may see him on the walls of the tomb, and subsequently
he married Ankhesenamun. We hear no more of Tutankhamen's widow.

Soon a new, vigorous dynasty, the Nineteenth (1350–
1200 B.C.) took the place of the old. The Pharaohs of this
period, men such as Sethos I, Ramesses II, and others, were
warriors who, in part, regained the empire which had almost been lost by Akhenaten and his short-lived successors. It is possible that at this time, when the very name
of the Heretic Pharaoh was obliterated from his monuments, that his descendants also fell into disfavor. Perhaps
even the records of their burials were destroyed; we do
not know.

Several attempts were made to rob Tutankhamen's
tomb; we have clear evidence of that. But such attempts
must have been made within a few years of the burial,
when the site of the tomb was known. Why was knowledge of its position forgotten after a time? Probably because the official records of these unpopular rulers, heirs,
and successors of Akhenaten, were deliberately expunged.
After that it was a matter of luck. Several generations

later, during the Twentieth Dynasty (1200–1090 B.C.) the enormous and elaborate tomb of Ramesses VI was cut out of the hillside immediately above the tomb of Tutankhamen. The stone chippings of the excavators poured down the valley slopes and effectively concealed the entrance to the modest sepulcher of this now-forgotten Pharaoh. And so, for three thousand years, it remained concealed, until one day, at a country house in England, Carter drew his patron's attention to a triangular area on the map and said "We *must* dig here."

Index